TOP 10 AMERICAN MEN'S OLYMPIC GOLD MEDALISTS

Ron Knapp

Enslow Publishers, Inc.

40 Industrial Road   PO Box 38
Box 398   Aldershot
Berkeley Heights, NJ 07922   Hants GU12 6BP
USA   UK

http://www.enslow.com

Dedication

For Room 2

Library of Congress Cataloging-in-Publication Data

Knapp, Ron.
    Top 10 American men's Olympic gold medalists / Ron Knapp.
       p. cm. — (Sports top 10)
    Includes bibliographical references and index.
    Summary: Profiles the lives and careers of Greg Barton, Dick Button, Eddie
Eagan, Eric Heiden, Greg Louganis, Billy Mills, Edwin Moses, Dan O'Brien,
Jesse Owens, and Mark Spitz.
    ISBN 0-7660-1274-3
    1. Athletes—Rating of—United States—Juvenile literature. 2. Olympics—
History—Juvenile literature. [1. Athletes. 2. Olympics—History.] I. Title:
American mens Olympic gold medalists. II. Title: Top ten American mens
Olympic gold medalists. III. Title: IV: Series.
GV697.A1 K59 2000
796'.092'2—dc21
  [B]   99-040389
                                        CIP

Printed in the United States of America

10 9 8 7 6 5 4 3 2 1

To Our Readers: All Internet addresses in this book were active and appropriate
when we went to press. Any comments or suggestions can be sent by e-mail to
Comments@enslow.com or to the address on the back cover.

Illustration Credits: AP/Wide World Photos, pp. 10, 15, 17, 19, 25, 26, 29;
© AAF 1992, pp. 35, 37; © AAF 1999, p. 21; © AAF/LPI 1984, pp. 22, 31, 33;
Photo by Ron Knapp, p. 6; United States Olympic Committee, pp. 13, 39,
41, 43, 45; USA/Canoe Kayak, p. 9.

Cover Illustration: © AAF/LPI 1984.

Cover Description: Olympic diver Greg Louganis.

Interior Design: Richard Stalzer

CONTENTS

Introduction

EVERY FOURTH SUMMER for more than a century, the world has focused its attention on its finest athletes. The modern Summer Olympic Games are the greatest sports spectacle on the planet. As of 1924, the Winter Olympic Games have also celebrated athletic talent.

Since the revival of the Games in the 1800s, some of their brightest stars have been Americans. These athletes have come from a wide variety of backgrounds. They grew up in large cities, small villages—and even on a hog farm.

The United States teams have been made up of whites as well as blacks and those such as Greg Louganis and Billy Mills, of Samoan and American Indian ancestry, respectively.

Most of these athletes were blessed with perfect bodies for their sports. Mark Spitz's huge hands and muscular legs helped propel him through the water like a torpedo. The long, powerful, yet agile body of Louganis made it possible for him to perform the leaps, twists, and turns that made him the most exciting diver in the world.

Many of these men were such gifted athletes that they could excel at more than one sport. Eddie Eagan was a gold-medal winner at both the Summer and Winter Games. After achieving Olympic glory in one sport, Edwin Moses and Eric Heiden each had great success at a different sport.

But excellence did not come easily to any of these men. Because of a birth defect, it took a series of operations to allow Greg Barton to walk. Jesse Owens had to continually fight against prejudice.

Of course, it takes more than just natural skills to be an Olympic champion. Besides their American citizenship, all ten of these athletes shared an intense determination to be the best in the world.

America has produced many outstanding Olympians.

Not everyone would agree that these men are ten of the best. Track and field legends Carl Lewis and Raymond Ewry, as well as swimmer Matt Biondi would be fine choices. Perhaps you can think of some other Olympic legends that have not been included. But by their achievements, these great athletes on *our* list made Americans proud and thrilled fans around the world.

OLYMPIC CAREER STATISTICS

Athlete	Year	Gold	Silver	Bronze	Event(s)
GREG BARTON	1984, 1988	2		2	1,000-meter individual kayak;
	1992				1,000-meter doubles kayak
DICK BUTTON	1948, 1952	2			Men's individual figure skating
EDDIE EAGAN	1920, 1932	2			Boxing, Light heavyweight div.;
					Four-man Bobsled
ERIC HEIDEN	1980	5			Speed skating, 500-, 1,000-,1,500-,
					5,000-, and 10,000-meter.
GREG LOUGANIS	1976, 1984	4	1		Springboard diving;
	1988				platform diving
BILLY MILLS	1964	1			10,000-meter race
EDWIN MOSES	1976, 1984	2		1	400-meter hurdles
	1988				
DAN O'BRIEN	1996	1			Decathlon
JESSE OWENS	1936	4			100-meter dash; 200-meter dash;
					4 x 100-meter relay; long jump
MARK SPITZ	1968, 1972	9	1	1	100- and 200-meter freestyle;
					100- and 200-meter butterfly;
					4 x 100-meter freestyle relay;
					4 x 200-meter freestyle relay;
					4 x 100-meter medley relay

GREG BARTON

Greg Barton overcame a birth defect known as clubfoot to become an Olympic champion.

GREG BARTON

GREG BARTON WAS BORN WITH TWO TWISTED FEET, a condition known as clubfoot. They were so twisted that if not for four operations he could never have learned to walk. For months, baby Greg had to wear two tiny casts. That was when his mother, Kathy, first noticed his toughness. Even with the casts, "he could creep faster than any baby I've ever seen."[1]

Barton recovered well enough to put in long hours at the family hog farm in Homer, Michigan. Because his feet still did not move perfectly, it was hard for him to develop much leg strength. However, that did not stop him from wrestling on his high school team.

Luckily for Barton, he discovered kayaking, a sport popular in Europe but then almost unknown in the United States. Athletes riding in light, seventeen-foot-long canoes paddle furiously through the water. It requires enormous arm strength, but very little from the feet or legs.

While attending the University of Michigan, Barton practiced kayaking regularly. After graduation, he became an engineer in California. Every day, before and after work, he carried his kayak to the water and raced for miles up and down the shores.

Barton became good enough to win world titles in 1985 and 1987, but hardly any Americans noticed. People who saw him practice in his strange-looking little boat had no idea they were watching a world champion. But Greg Barton did not kayak for glory. All he wanted was "personal satisfaction, seeing if I can be the best. Beyond that, I just like the feeling of being in a boat and feeling it accelerate through the water."[2]

Barton was one of nine men who qualified for the 1,000-meter singles finals at the 1988 Seoul Olympics. After a slow start, he was seventh at the 250-meter mark. Then he poured it on. At 750 meters, he was second and closing in on Grant Davies of Australia.

Barton and Davies crossed the finish line together! Nobody knew who had won. After carefully examining photos of the race, officials finally determined Barton had won by a centimeter. He had finished five thousandths of a second ahead of Davies.

But Barton had no time to celebrate. He was minutes away from competing with Norm Bellingham in the 1,000-meter doubles.

With 250 meters left, the Americans were third. By then, Bellingham was exhausted. "I was so scared," he said. "I looked over and we were a boat length behind . . . I just totally relied on Greg."[3]

Once again, Barton came through. He and Bellingham slipped past the competition, winning by twenty-nine hundredths of a second. In less than ninety minutes, Barton had won two Olympic gold medals!

By the time he returned home with his medals, Greg Barton was a celebrity. Thousands lined the streets to cheer as he rode past on a wagon pulled by horses. Then they waited in line at Homer High School for his autograph.

For a while, Barton was no longer an anonymous athlete in an unknown sport. Not only had he won the United States' first Olympic kayaking medal, he had taken two golds by a combined margin of less than a third of a second! And millions of Americans had been introduced to an exciting new sport.

GREG BARTON

BORN: December 12, 1959, Jackson, Michigan.

COLLEGE: University of Michigan.

EVENT(S): Kayak, 1,000-meter individual and 1,000-meter doubles.

RECORDS/MEDALS: Gold-medal winner, 1,000-meter individual kayak, 1988 Olympics; gold-medal winner, 1,000-meter kayak doubles, 1988 Olympics; bronze-medal winner 1,000-meter individual kayak, 1984 and 1992 Olympics.

HONORS: A small circular park in his hometown was named in his honor, Greg Barton Circle.

Slicing through the water, Barton rows his kayak to victory.

Internet Address
http://www.voyager.co.nz/~delmak/gregbarton.html

DICK BUTTON

Dick Button brought an exciting style and flair to men's figure skating. He was one of the first skaters to make dangerous jumps a part of his routine.

DICK BUTTON

FOR THE BUTTON BROTHERS, GEORGE AND JACK, skating was just something fun to do in the winter. Their little brother, Dick, took their outgrown skates and decided he wanted it to be something more. He loved skating so much that he wanted to compete.

Dick Button's first coach told him to forget that idea. At five-feet two-inches tall, and 160 pounds, the twelve-year-old Button had too much weight and too little talent. The boy and his parents did not listen; he got a new coach and kept skating.

Gustave Luissi, a former ski jumper from Switzerland, had some unusual ideas for his pupils. He wanted them to jump high and long. Until then, all skaters had concentrated on making perfect patterns on the ice. Exciting jumps were not considered an important part of figure skating.

Button loved to jump—and he loved to practice. Fortunately, he began to grow taller and thinner. Soon he was competing against the country's best skaters. At his first important meet, he was runner-up. That was not good enough. "I want to be first, not second," he said.[1] He practiced even harder.

By the time he was sixteen, in 1946, Button was the United States' youngest national champion. He also won the title each of the next six years.

Until then, men's skating had been dominated by Europeans. They did not know what to make of Button's moves. He seemed to be jumping and spinning all over the rink. Was this skating or some weird new kind of acrobatics on skates? The fans loved his flashy style, and soon the other skaters were copying his moves.

For the 1948 Winter Olympics in St. Moritz, Switzerland, Button wanted to dazzle the world with a brand-new move. He had been practicing the difficult two-and-a-half-revolution double axle jump for months, but it just was not working. He kept landing poorly and sprawling on the ice. Finally, two days before the Olympic competition began, he nailed the move in practice. He was able to perform it beautifully in front of the judges, and he won the gold medal!

Four years later, Button wanted another new move for the Olympic Games in Oslo, Norway. This time the move was a triple jump. Over and over he jumped and fell. But he kept practicing, and six weeks before the 1952 competition he perfected the difficult jump in practice. When he hit it at the Olympics, he had his second gold medal.

Dick Button had become the most exciting and important figure skater the United States had ever produced. He made the sport very popular in his country. His wild, daring style transformed figure skating around the world. It became the thrilling sport it is today.

"He was fantastic," said Kurt Browning, a world champion decades after Button retired. "He was an incredible skater. He had wonderful agility, and when it came to jumps, he was far ahead of his time."[2]

DICK BUTTON

BORN: July 18, 1929, Englewood, New Jersey.

COLLEGE: Harvard University.

EVENT(S): Figure Skating.

RECORDS/MEDALS: U. S. Senior Men's Champion, 1946–1952; North American Men's Champion, 1947, 1949, 1951; European Champion, 1948; World Champion, 1948–1952; gold-medal winner for individual men's figure skating, 1948, 1952; only person to ever hold all five of these titles at once, 1948.

HONORS: Sullivan Award winner (best amateur athlete), 1949; won Emmy Award as best television analyst, 1980–1981 season; inducted into the U.S. Olympic Hall of Fame, 1983.

Button is credited with making men's figure skating popular in the United States.

Internet Address

http://www.olympic-usa.org/olympians/meet/bios/figureskating/button.html

EDDIE EAGAN

AFTER HER HUSBAND, JOHN, WAS KILLED in a railroad accident, Clara Eagan had to raise her son, Eddie, and his four brothers alone. She supported her boys by teaching French and German. She was an accomplished linguist who could speak five languages. Education was very important to Clara Eagan and her sons.

Eddie Eagan was a fine athlete who loved all sports. By the time he was in high school, he was an excellent boxer— maybe even good enough to become a professional champion. Instead, he went to one of the country's most prestigious schools, Yale University.

While attending classes, he continued to box. In 1919, he competed in the Amateur Athletic Union (AAU) Championships in two weight classes. It was a grueling tournament; he had seven fights in two days. Hours after losing the light heavyweight title, he won the heavyweight championship.

The following year, he joined the American team in Antwerp, Belgium, for the Olympics. He earned a gold medal by taking the light heavyweight division.

Many fighters have gone straight from the Olympics into pro boxing, but not Eddie Eagan. He went back to Yale. Then after graduating, he went to law school at Harvard University and then at Oxford University in England. He continued to box but remained an amateur; he was never paid. Eagan became the first American to win the British amateur championship.

After earning his law degree, "he and a friend took a trip around the world," said his wife, Peggy. "In every country

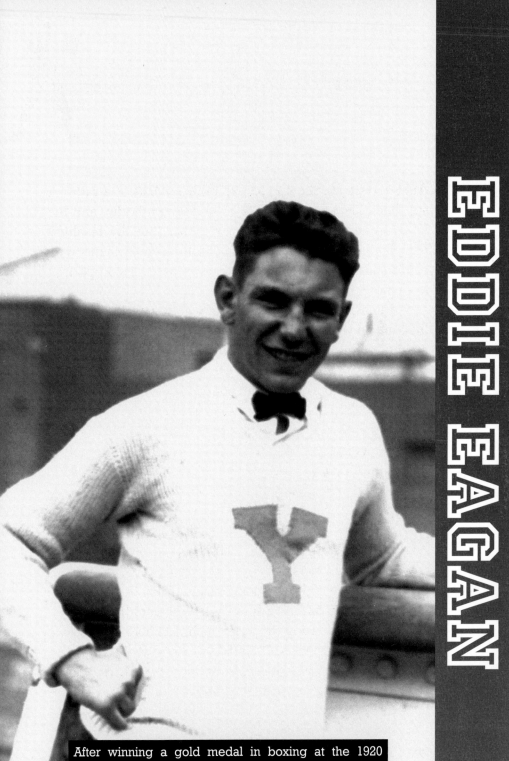

After winning a gold medal in boxing at the 1920 Olympics, Eddie Eagan returned to Yale University.

EDDIE EAGAN

Eddie challenged the amateur champion. He finished the tour undefeated."[1] The trip lasted two years. Then, Eagan settled down and became a lawyer back in the United States.

A few years later, the United States Winter Olympic squad was in trouble. The weather had been too warm to hold tryouts for the bobsled team, and there were only three athletes signed up for the four-man team. Soon the 1932 Winter Olympic Games would begin in Lake Placid, New York.

The team was so desperate that they called on Eagan, by then a thirty-three-year-old lawyer. "Guess what," he told Peggy. "I'm on the United States bobsled team."[2] So what if he had never been on a bobsled? "Eddie was absolutely fearless," his wife remembered. "He would try everything just for the thrill of it. Besides, they could find nobody else. Without Eddie, there would be no team. After a few practice sessions they performed like they had been together for years."[3]

Bobsledding is a dangerous sport. After pushing their sled to a running start, the four men jumped in and shot downhill. A mistake at top speed would send them crashing off the track. "Picture a steel comet with four riders hurtling through the air," Eagan said.

On their final run, on a sharp, dangerous curve, one of their runners almost went off the track. But the team held on and defeated the second-place squad by two seconds. Eddie Eagan had his second gold medal!

BORN: April 26, 1898, Denver, Colorado.

DIED: June 14, 1967.

COLLEGE: Yale University, Harvard University, Oxford University.

EVENT(S): Boxing, Light Heavyweight Division; 4-man Bobsled.

RECORDS/MEDALS: Won gold medal, lightheavyweight boxing, 1920 Olympics; won gold medal, 4-man bobsled, 1932 Olympics; only man to ever win a gold medal at both the Summer and Winter Olympics.

HONORS: Inducted into the U.S. Olympic Hall of Fame, 1983.

After retiring from competitions, Eddie Eagan became the chairman of the New York State Athletic Commission. With him are boxers Jake LaMotta (right), and Marcel Cerdan (left).

Internet Address

http://www.olympic-usa.org/games/ga_2_5_28.html

ERIC HEIDEN

WHEN ERIC HEIDEN WAS JUST TWO years old, his father, Jack, took him skating. Over and over the little boy fell on the ice. "I'm too little to skate," he finally said.[1]

But soon Eric Heiden was big enough, and he discovered he loved the feeling of gliding over the ice. When he was just thirteen, Diane Holum, a champion speed skater, became his coach. If Heiden was willing to work hard enough, she thought, he could be a champion, too.

The teenager began spending hours every day on the ice. He also lifted weights, sprinted, repeatedly ran up and down dozens of steps, and rode thousands of miles on his bicycle. Holum also had him duckwalk for miles, pulling her behind him. The workouts were all designed to improve his endurance and strengthen his thighs.

There are five speed-skating events in the Olympics. Some athletes concentrate on the short sprints of 500 and 1,000 meters. The distance skaters compete in the 5,000- and 10,000-meter events. The other race, 1,500 meters, is usually considered too long for the sprinters and too short for the distance experts. Heiden did not want to specialize; he would compete in all five events.

In 1976, at the Innsbruck Olympics, when he was seventeen, he finished nineteenth in the 5,000-meter event and seventh in the 1,500-meter event. Of course, he kept working. The next year, he became the first American ever to take the overall title in the World Speed Skating Championships. Heiden would compete for three more years, and he would never again be defeated.

At the 1980 Olympics in Lake Placid, New York, he

ERIC HEIDEN

Moving quickly around the corner, Eric Heiden tries to put some more distance between him and the pack during the race for the 10,000-meter gold medal.

entered all five events. In the 500-meter event, he was matched against Yevgeny Kulikov, the world-record holder. After falling behind, Heiden stormed back to win by inches.

In the 5,000-meter event the next day, he again fell behind, but his strong finish clinched the victory. As the competition went on, Heiden seemed to get even stronger. He beat everybody by a second and a half in the 1,000-meter event.

Early in the 1,500-meter race, his skate caught on a rut in the ice, and he almost fell, but he still won by more than a second. Then in the longest event, the 10,000 meters, he astonished the screaming fans by clocking 14:28.13, an incredible time that cut 6.2 seconds off the world record.

Eric Heiden became the only Olympic athlete to win five individual gold medals—and then he retired from his sport. For the next seven years, he competed as a professional bicycle racer in Europe and in the United States. In 1985, he was the United States champion.

Finally, Heiden gave up competitive cycling after a bad crash. He enrolled in medical school, and today he is a doctor. Among the patients he has treated are the players for the NBA's Sacramento Kings and the Sacramento Monarchs of the WNBA.

ERIC HEIDEN

BORN: June 14, 1958, Madison, Wisconsin.

COLLEGE: Stanford University.

EVENT(S): 500-meter, 1,000-meter, 1,500-meter, 5,000-meter, and 10,000-meter speed skating.

RECORDS/MEDALS: World junior speed skating champion, 1977–1979; won gold medal, 500-meter, 1,000-meter, 1,500-meter, 5,000-meter, and 10,000-meter speed skating, 1980 Olympics; first person to ever win the gold medal in all five speed skating events.

HONORS: USOC Sportsman of the Year, 1977, 1979–1980; UPI International Male Athlete of the Year, 1980; Sullivan Award, 1980; Jesse Owens International Trophy, 1981; inducted into the U.S. Olympic Hall of Fame, 1983.

Eric Heiden poses for a picture with his coach, Olympic speed skater Diane Holum.

Internet Address

http://www.olympic-usa.org/olympians/meet/bios/speedska/heiden.html

GREG LOUGANIS

When Louganis had problems growing up, he focused his energy on diving. Eventually, he became the best diver in the world.

GREG LOUGANIS

WHEN THE DARK-SKINNED SAMOAN Greg Louganis was a baby, he was adopted by a white California couple. "Mom said that what really clinched the deal was my smile. Once she saw that, she didn't want to look at any other babies," he said.[1]

School was tough for Louganis. He had dyslexia, which made it very hard for him to read. He was a fine athlete, though. During recess, he played volleyball, kickball, and softball. But what he really enjoyed was dancing and diving. That made many of his classmates laugh. They called him a sissy. They also made fun of his dark skin and called him a dummy. Many times they beat him up.

Of course, Greg Louganis was miserable at school. He began taking his anger out on his parents. His mother, Frances, had to call the police after he attacked her. Greg began abusing marijuana and alcohol.

Despite his problems, his mother stuck by him. She encouraged his dancing and diving. Louganis tried to quit listening to the taunts of his classmates. "I learned to focus most of that angry energy on my acrobatics and diving."[2]

Louganis's body was perfectly suited to diving. He was an agile youngster who could easily twist his body into a variety of shapes. His legs were incredibly strong, which allowed him to leap high in the air, gaining extra time to complete his moves.

When Louganis was eleven, he was awarded a perfect ten as a diver at the 1971 Junior Olympics. Five years later, he barely lost the platform diving gold medal to Italy's Klaus Dibiasi at the 1976 Olympics in Montreal. "I'm disappointed, sure," said his coach, Dr. Sammy Lee, "but no one is going to touch Greg in the future."[3]

After the American boycott of the 1980 Moscow Olympics, Louganis won his first gold medal by dominating the springboard diving competition at the 1984 Los Angeles games. A week later, as he stood on the platform before his final dive in that event, he thought, "No matter what I do, my mother is still going to love me."[4] The dive was almost perfect! Louganis was the first male athlete in fifty-six years to sweep both diving events.

In preliminary competition at the 1988 Seoul Games, Louganis did not jump high enough, and his head banged the springboard on the way down. After getting four stitches, he returned to the board and won another gold.

Then in the platform event, with one dive left, he was behind Xiong Ni, a fourteen-year-old Chinese diver. Louganis chose to do a dangerous reverse three-and-a-half somersault in the tuck position. Because two other divers attempting it had been fatally injured by slamming their heads onto the board, it was called the Dive of Death.

Louganis walked slowly, calmly to the edge of the board—and nailed the dive! He narrowly beat Ni for his fourth gold medal and his second Olympic diving sweep.

After retiring from competition, Louganis appeared onstage as a dancer and an actor. He also took an active role in AIDS prevention, and told people about his struggles for acceptance as an athlete who is homosexual. He surprised his fans by revealing that he was HIV-positive when he won his last two Olympic medals in 1988.

GREG LOUGANIS

BORN: January 29, 1960, El Cajon, California.

COLLEGE: University of Miami-Florida; University of California-Irvine.

EVENT(S): Springboard Diving, Platform Diving.

RECORDS/MEDALS: Olympic gold-medal winner, platform diving, 1984, 1988; Olympic gold-medal winner, springboard diving, 1984, 1988; Olympic silver-medal winner, platform diving, 1976.

HONORS: USOC Sportsman of the Year, 1982, 1987; Sullivan Award winner, 1984; inducted into the U.S. Olympic Hall of Fame, 1985; Jesse Owens International Trophy, 1987; Olympic Spirit Award, 1988; "Wide World of Sports" Athlete of the Year, 1988; inducted into the International Swimming Hall of Fame, 1993.

In 1984, Louganis became the first male athlete in fifty-six years to win both the platform and springboard diving competitions.

Internet Address
http://www.olympic-usa.org/olympians/meet/bios/diving/louganis.html

BILLY MILLS

Going into the 10,000-meter run, nobody thought that Billy Mills had a chance to win. Here he is shown crossing the finish line.

AT THE 1964 OLYMPICS IN TOKYO, Australian Ron Clarke was almost always surrounded by reporters. After all, he was the favorite to win the 10,000-meter run.

One of them asked if he was worried about Billy Mills. "Worry about him?" said Clarke. "I never heard of him."[1]

Clarke was not the only one. Before the race not a single reporter talked to Mills. He was not even the fastest American entered in the event. Nobody thought he had a chance. He would be lucky to finish in the first ten.

But Billy Mills had been running all his life—and he loved it. He was an American Indian, a Lakota Sioux who had grown up on a reservation in South Dakota. Twice, he was the state high school mile champion. At the University of Kansas, he was captain of the cross-country team.

His wife, Pat, talked him into trying out for the United States Olympic team. Even if he could not win, he would enjoy the competition and the trip to Tokyo. Mills made the team, but his best time was almost a minute behind Clarke's world-record 28:15.6.

"My strategy was simply to go out with the top four runners . . . and hope for the best," Mills said. Halfway through the race, that's just where he was. "I was within one second of my fastest 5,000 meters ever and there was still 5,000 meters to go!"[2]

"I was thinking that I couldn't continue at this pace . . . The leaders started pulling away from me. I thought that I might just as well let them go."[3]

But then he thought, "Hey, wait a minute." Maybe he could hang on a little longer. "So I started fighting back, slowly coming up on them . . . If I had to quit I wasn't going to do it in front of where Pat was sitting."[4]

Finally only two runners had a chance to take Clarke—Mills and Tunisia's Mohamed Gammoudi. "Clarke looked back, saw Gammoudi and me, and was worried. From that point on, I stayed with him."[5]

As the final lap started, Mills passed Clarke. All three leaders had to make their way through the slower runners they were lapping.

Clarke suddenly shoved his way past Mills, who stumbled. Then Gammoundi raced past both of them, but Mills did not quit. "Something inside me was saying, 'There's still a chance.' . . . So I started driving. They were fifteen yards in front of me, but it seemed like 50 yards. Then I kept telling myself, 'I can win . . . I can win . . .' and the next thing I remember I broke the tape."[6]

A Japanese official ran up to him and asked, "Who are you?"[7]

But by then, the huge stadium crowd and millions more watching on television knew who he was. He was Billy Mills, winner of the gold medal in one of the most thrilling upsets in sports history. His time of 28:24.4 was 46 seconds faster than he had ever run before.

BILLY MILLS

BORN: June 30, 1938, Pine Ridge Indian Reservation, South Dakota.

COLLEGE: University of Kansas.

EVENT(S): Track and Field, 10,000-meter race.

RECORDS/MEDALS: Olympic gold-medal winner, 10,000-meter race, 1964.

HONORS: Inducted into the USA Track and Field Hall of Fame, 1976; inducted into the U.S. Olympic Hall of Fame, 1984.

Mills waves to the crowd while on the podium to accept his medal. To the left is the silver-medal-winner Mohamed Gammoudi of Tunisia, and to the right is Ron Clarke of Australia.

Internet Address

http://www.olympic-usa.org/olympians/meet/bios/track&field/mills.html

EDWIN MOSES

AS A YOUNGSTER, EDWIN MOSES was a fine athlete. He was an all-star catcher in Little League and a defensive back on his high school football team. When he was just five-feet eight-inches tall, he could jump high enough to dunk a basketball.

However, his favorite sport was track and field. He had loved it ever since he watched a meet in his hometown of Dayton, Ohio when he was in third grade.

But the most important thing in the Moses household was education, not sports. Little Edwin loved his children's encyclopedia. By the time he was seven years old, he had read it all the way through from A to Z.

Moses earned an academic scholarship to Morehouse College, where he studied physics and engineering. As a member of the school's track team, he turned in a fine time of 50.1 seconds in the 400-meter intermediate hurdles. That was early in 1976, just before the Montreal Olympics.

Moses studied his event just as he studied physics. He decided he would take only thirteen steps, not fifteen like everybody else, between hurdles. To do that, he had to have an incredibly long stride. Each step moved him nine feet nine inches. He came up with a training program that included long-distance running, yoga, and martial arts as well as work on the track.

His time had improved to 48.30, an American record, at the United States Trials. Then, at the Olympics, he set a world record of 47.64 as he took the gold medal.

Over the next decade, Moses dominated the event. "I know I'm the man to beat whenever I go out on the track,"

Edwin Moses takes the lead in the 400-meter hurdles at the 1984 Olympic Games.

he said. "I've always gone into my races more prepared than anyone else."[1] His best performance—47.02—came on August 31, 1983, his twenty-eighth birthday.

Moses missed the 1980 Olympics in Moscow because of a boycott by the American team. He was still favored to win four years later in Los Angeles.

After fifty yards, he was ahead to stay. "I could feel I was moving away from the others," he said.[2] He had his second gold medal.

What brought Moses more attention than his medals and record times was what became known as The Streak. From 1977 until 1987, he won 122 consecutive races. At one point, he was responsible for eighteen of the nineteen fastest 400-meter hurdle times ever run. For almost a decade, nobody could touch him. He was such an accomplished, popular athlete that thousands of fans showed up just to watch him practice.

After retiring from track, Moses became a bobsledder. He was good enough to be part of a team that won a World Cup medal.

Edwin Moses has always encouraged athletes to work hard both at practice and in school. "Education has been the key to my whole life," he said. "If I had not gotten a scholarship and gone to Morehouse . . . no one would have known who I was."[3]

EDWIN MOSES

BORN: August 31, 1955, Dayton, Ohio.

COLLEGE: Morehouse College, Atlanta, Georgia.

EVENT(S): 400-meter hurdles.

RECORDS/AWARDS: Olympic gold-medal winner, 400-meter hurdles, 1976, 1984; Olympic bronze-medal winner, 400-meter hurdles, 1988.

HONORS: Sullivan Award winner, 1983; Jesse Owens International Trophy, 1984; USOC Sportsman of the Year, 1984; "Wide World of Sports" Athlete of the Year, 1984; inducted into the U.S. Olympic Hall of Fame, 1985; selected as a member of the 1991 United States bobsled team; inducted into the USA Track and Field Hall of Fame, 1994.

From 1977 to 1987, Edwin Moses won 122 consecutive races.

Internet Address

http://www.olympic-usa.org/olympians/meet/bios/track&field/moses.html

DAN O'BRIEN

WHEN HE WAS JUST THREE years old, Dan O'Brien's father watched him race around the family farm in Klamath Falls, Oregon. "Boy, can he run," said the proud man. "He's gonna be in the Olympics someday!"[1]

Until he was adopted by Jim and Virginia O'Brien, Dan spent the first two years of his life in foster homes. Five of the O'Briens' seven children were adopted. They had a variety of backgrounds—Korean, American Indian, and Hispanic. Dan O'Brien is African American and Finnish.

Because of his attention deficit disorder, Dan had a tough time in school. His parents always encouraged him to keep trying. "I never gave up," he said later, "no matter how hard the struggle."[2]

O'Brien was a star at football, baseball, and track. At the Oregon State AA High School Meet, he won the 100-meter dash, 110-meter hurdles, 300-meter dash, and the long jump. He outscored all the other teams by himself.

Coach Mike Keller gave O'Brien a scholarship to the University of Idaho. O'Brien had a chance to be a big college star, but he blew it by partying too much. He was arrested for drunk driving, lost his scholarship, and flunked out.

Keller, and Jim and Virginia O'Brien stuck by Dan as he put his life back together. He got a job and earned enough money to go back to school. He studied, passed his classes, and graduated.

He also began concentrating on the decathlon, a tough competition that lasts two days. Athletes have to run 100-meter, 400-meter, and 1,500-meter races, as well as the

DAN O'BRIEN

From the time he was young, decathlete Dan O'Brien was a multitalented athlete. In high school, he excelled at football, baseball, and track.

110-meter hurdles. They also have to compete in the broad jump, high jump, discus, shot put, javelin, and pole vault. The winner is the athlete who earns the most total points. It's an incredibly tough contest; the world champion decathlete is considered the world's greatest athlete. "You run until you almost throw up three or four times a week . . . and you get into this feeling that you could just run forever. You feel like a superman sometimes," O'Brien said.[3]

By 1991, he was the world champion and a favorite to win the 1992 Olympic competition in Barcelona, Spain. The Reebok shoe company made him the center of a $25 million advertising campaign. But O'Brien missed all three of his pole vault attempts at the Olympic Trials and did not even make the team. Instead, he went to Barcelona as a television commentator.

A month later, he set a world decathlon record of 8,891 points. He also won the World Championship in 1993 and 1995. "I can say I'm the greatest athlete," he said, "but it doesn't mean anything without the Olympic gold medal. To win gold means that you're the world's greatest athlete."[4]

In 1996, O'Brien easily qualified for the American team. After nine events in Atlanta, he was ahead by only 71 points. Because of the complicated scoring system, the athlete with the best chance to beat him was Germany's Frank Busemann, who was 209 points behind. The final event was one of Busemann's best, the 1,500-meter run. It was one of O'Brien's poorest, the one he likes the least. If the German could beat him by thirty seconds, Busemann, not O'Brien, would get the gold.

Busemann knew what he had to do; he took off like a bullet. O'Brien sank farther and farther behind. But he did not give up, and he finally started to close the gap. Busemann got to the finish line first—and collapsed.

Just fourteen and a half seconds later, O'Brien was there as well. Finally, he was an Olympic champion.

Dan O'Brien

BORN: July 18, 1966, Portland, Oregon.

COLLEGE: University of Idaho.

EVENT(S): Decathlon.

RECORDS/MEDALS: Broke American record with 8,812 points at the World Championships, Tokyo, Japan, 1991: broke world record with 8,891 points at DecaStar Meet in Talence, France, 1992; decathlon World Champion, 1991, 1993, 1995; won silver medal at Goodwill Games, 1990; won gold medal at Goodwill Games, 1994, 1998; gold-medal winner, decathlon, 1996 Olympic Games.

After his disappointment at the 1992 Olympic Trials, O'Brien rebounded in 1996 to make the team, and win the gold medal.

Internet Address

http://www.usatf.org/athletes/bios/obrien.shtml

JESSE OWENS

ONE OF JESSE OWENS'S FIRST track coaches told him to run "like the ground was a burning fire."[1]

But Owens could do more than just blaze down the track; he could also fly. When he was still a youngster, he held world junior high school records for the long jump and the high jump.

At the 1935 Big Ten Championships, Owens had the greatest hour in the history of track. In less than sixty minutes, he set world records in the 220-yard sprint, long jump, and 220-yard low hurdles, and tied another in the 100-yard dash.

Owens faced a big disadvantage; he was an African American competing in a white world. Legal discrimination and prejudice severely limited opportunities for African Americans in all areas of society, not just sports. Aside from boxing, they were not allowed to compete in any professional major-league sports. Many colleges did not welcome them, either. In fact, when Owens was named captain of the Ohio State University track team, he was the first African-American captain in the Big Ten.

Owens is best remembered for his magnificent performance in the 1936 Olympics in Berlin, Germany. Adolf Hitler, the Nazi leader, was the ruler of Germany. He preached the superiority of the white race; he certainly did not want to see Jesse Owens do well in the Nazi capital in front of the whole world.

On the way to Germany, Jesse dreamed of "taking one or two of those gold medals."[2] He did much more than that.

Of course, not all whites were against him. In the

JESSE OWENS

Lunging through the air, Jesse Owens competes in the long-jump competition. Owens won four gold medals at the 1936 Olympics.

qualifying competition for the long jump, Owens had blown his first two attempts by stepping over the foul line. If he missed his third attempt, he was finished. That's when "the German champion Luz Long saved me."[3] Long put his towel a foot in front of the line and told Owens to jump from that spot. It worked. Owens qualified, then won the gold medal with a jump of 26 feet 5.5 inches. The silver medalist—and the first man to congratulate him—was Long.

After Owens also took gold in the 100-meter dash in 10.3 seconds, a light rain did not stop him from winning the 200-meter dash in 20.7 seconds.

Finally, he was part of the world-record-setting foursome that took the 4 x 100 meter relay in 39.8 seconds. Jesse Owens left Berlin with four gold medals!

Until his death forty-four years later, Owens was one of the world's most popular Olympic champions. He gave advice freely to the athletes who were breaking his records, and he encouraged hundreds of thousands of young people with pep talks, challenging them to do their best at everything they tried.

And Owens was never bitter about the discrimination he had faced. Despite our country's problems, he said, "in America, anyone can become somebody."[4]

JESSE OWENS

BORN: September 12, 1913, Danville, Alabama.

DIED: March 31, 1980.

COLLEGE: Ohio State University.

EVENT(S): 100-meter dash; 200-meter dash; 4 x 100-meter relay; long jump.

RECORDS/MEDALS: Broke 5 world records in one afternoon at Big Ten Championships, May 25, 1935; gold-medal winner, 100-meter dash, 1936 Olympic Games; gold-medal winner, 200-meter dash, 1936 Olympic Games; gold-medal winner, 4 x 100-meter relay, 1936 Olympics; gold-medal winner, long jump, 1936 Olympics.

HONORS: Associated Press Male Athlete of the Year, 1936; inducted into the USA Track and Field Hall of Fame, 1974; received the Presidential Medal of Freedom, 1976; inducted into the U.S. Olympic Hall of Fame, 1983.

Jesse Owens was one of the most popular American Olympians until his death in 1980. He is one of few Americans to have received the Presidential Medal of Freedom.

Internet Address

http://www.usatf.org/athletes/hof/owens.shtml

MARK SPITZ

WHEN MARK SPITZ WAS TWO years old, he loved to splash in the beautiful warm water at Waikiki Beach in Honolulu, Hawaii. Four years later, after the family moved to California, Arnold Spitz rowed his son to the cold water near San Francisco Bay. Jump in, he told him. Learn to swim.

Mark Spitz was a fast learner. By the time his father rowed him home, he could swim. Four years later, he was the fastest ten-year-old butterfly-stroke swimmer in the nation. By the time he was sixteen, he was the national champion in the 100-meter butterfly.

Mark Spitz was lucky. He had a perfect body for a swimmer. He was long and thin and strong. He also had huge hands that could push large amounts of water. And his knees could flex forward slightly to give him a stronger kick. Besides that, he was willing to work very hard. Many days he spent five to six hours practicing in the water.

His parents encouraged him to be the best. "Swimming isn't everything," his father kept telling him. "Winning is."[1]

By the 1968 Mexico City Olympics, Spitz was good enough and confident enough that he predicted he would win as many as five or six gold medals. Many fans and swimmers thought he was bragging. They were happy when Spitz only took two gold medals in relay events.

He was disappointed, but he returned to his heavy practice schedule. Next time, he vowed, he would do better. He made a genuine effort to stop bragging and to get along with his teammates on the Indiana University team.

But by 1972, Spitz was in superb shape, and he could

MARK SPITZ

Mark Spitz was disappointed when he won only two gold medals at the 1968 Olympics. In 1972, Spitz won seven gold medals in one of the most dominating performances in sports history.

not help predicting that he was going to win seven gold medals at the Munich Olympics.

In his first event, after cruising to an easy win in the 200-meter butterfly, Spitz jumped out of the water and raised his big hands high in the air. His time was 2:00.7, a world record.

A few hours later he swam the anchor leg of the 4 x 100-meter freestyle. The American's time of 3:26.42 was good enough for gold and a world record.

The next day, in the 200-meter freestyle, he trailed teammate Steven Genter with just 50 meters to go, but passed him for the gold in a record-setting 1:52.78.

A day later in the 100-meter butterfly, his 54:27 was good enough for gold and another record. Hours later, he won another gold and set another record anchoring the 4 x 100-meter relay in 3:26.42.

At the finish of the 100-meter freestyle, fellow American Jerry Heidenreich closed strong but finished a half stroke behind Spitz's record pace of 51:22.

Then in the 4 x 100-meter medley, the American team's time of 3:48.16 beat the competition by almost four seconds. Seven events. Seven gold medals. Seven world records.

Soon a poster of Spitz in his swimming trunks wearing his seven medals sold millions of copies. But he was much more proud of a photograph of his teammates lifting him to their shoulders after his final victory.

"Having a tribute from your teammates is a feeling that can never be duplicated."[2]

Mark Spitz

BORN: February 10, 1950, Modesto, California.

COLLEGE: Indiana University.

EVENT(S): Swimming, 100-meter freestyle; 200-meter freestyle; 100-meter butterfly; 200-meter butterfly; 4 x 100-meter freestyle relay; 4 x 200-meter freestyle relay; 4 x 100-meter medley relay.

RECORDS/MEDALS: Gold-medal winner, 4 x 100-meter freestyle relay, 1968, 1972; gold-medal winner 4 x 200-meter freestyle relay, 1968, 1972; gold-medal winner, 4 x 100-meter medley relay; gold-medal winner, 100-meter freestyle, 1972; gold-medal winner, 200-meter freestyle, 1972; gold-medal winner, 100-meter butterfly, 1972; gold-medal winner, 200-meter butterfly, 1972; first person to win seven gold medals in one Olympic games, 1972.

HONORS: Sullivan Award, 1971; Associated Press Male Athlete of the Year, 1972; inducted into the International Swimming Hall of Fame, 1977; inducted into the U.S. Olympic Hall of Fame, 1983.

Spitz set seven world records at the 1972 Olympics. After the games, he became a celebrity, appearing on many television variety and talk shows.

Internet Address

http://www.olympic-usa.org/olympians/meet/bios/swimming/spitz.html

CHAPTER NOTES

Greg Barton

1. Rick Telander, "A Yank Who Makes Waves," *Sports Illustrated*, vol. 69, September 14, 1988, p. 76.

2. Ibid.

3. Crosbie Cotton, "Picture Perfect: Greg Barton Won Two Golds in Photo Finishes," *Sports Illustrated*, vol. 69, October 10, 1988, p. 115.

Dick Button

1. Art Berke, ed., *Lincoln Library of Sports Champions* (Columbus, Ohio: Frontier Press Company, 1985), vol. 3, p. 57.

2. Mark Kram, "Dick Button Is a Pioneer, Educator of Figure Skating," Knight-Ridder/Tribune News Service, January 2, 1998.

Eddie Eagan

1. Brad Herzog, "Modeled on a Myth," *Sports Illustrated*, vol. 87, December 29, 1997, p. 8.

2. Ibid.

3. Ibid.

Eric Heiden

1. Art Berke, ed., *Lincoln Library of Sports Champions* (Columbus, Ohio: Frontier Press Company, 1985), vol. 8, p. 38.

Greg Louganis

1. Greg Louganis with Eric Marcus, *Breaking the Surface* (New York: Random House, 1995), p. 28.

2. Ibid., p. 38.

3. Steve Bisheff, "Louganis Was More Like an Artist Than an Athlete," Knight-Ridder/Tribune News Service, February 24, 1995.

4. David Wallechinsky, *The Complete Book of the Summer Olympics* (Boston: Little, Brown, and Company, 1996), p. 360.

Billy Mills

1. C. Robert Paul and Jack Orr, *The Olympic Games from Ancient Greece to Mexico City* (New York: The Lion Press, 1968), p. 129.

2. Bud Greenspan, *100 Greatest Moments in Olympic History* (Los Angeles: General Publishing Group, 1995), p. 89.

3. Lewis H. Carlson and John J. Fogarty, *Tales of Gold* (Chicago: Contemporary Books, Inc., 1987), p. 350.

4. Ibid.

5. Ibid., p. 351.

6. Greenspan, p. 89.

7. Ibid.

Edwin Moses

1. Art Berke, ed., *Lincoln Library of Sports Champions* (Columbus, Ohio: Frontier Press Company, 1985), vol. 12, p. 110.

2. Bud Greenspan, *100 Greatest Moments in Olympic History* (Los Angeles: General Publishing Group, Inc., 1995), p. 59.

3. "Former Olympian Edwin Moses Says Education Key to His Success," *Jet*, vol. 90, July 22, 1996, p. 18.

Dan O'Brien

1. "The Beginning," *Dan O'Brien Timeline*, n.d., <http://www.danobrien.com/timeline.htm> (February 10, 1999).

2. Claudia Hutchinson, "Oregon's Famous Adoptee," *Dan's Adoption*, November 1996, <http://darkwing.uoregon.edu/~obrien/dan.bio1.html> (February 10, 1999).

3. Ibid.

4. Michael Bauman, "Halfway home, O'Brien first," *On Wisconsin Sports*, August 1, 1996, <http://www.onwis.com/sports/oly/dec731.html> (February 10, 1999).

Jesse Owens

1. Brad Herzog, *The Sports 100* (New York: Macmillan, 1995), p. 135.

2. Ibid., p. 136.

3. Bud Greenspan, *100 Greatest Moments in Olympic History* (Los Angeles: General Publishing Group, Inc., 1995), p. 19.

4. Herzog, p. 135.

Mark Spitz

1. David Wallechinsky, *The Complete Book of the Summer Olympics* (Boston: Little, Brown and Company, 1996), p. 616.

2. Bud Greenspan, *100 Greatest Moments in Olympic History* (Los Angeles: General Publishing Group, Inc., 1995), p. 196.

INDEX

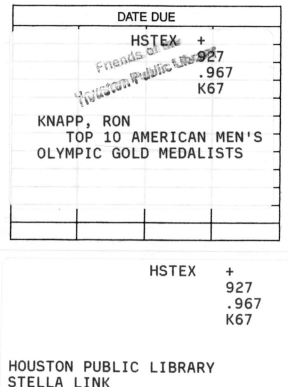